CW00854984

HOW TO BECOME A FEMME FATALE : THE ULTIMATE GUIDE TO SEDUCTION

AURNY AIRDUVAL

HOW TO BECOME A FEMME FATALE : THE ULTIMATE GUIDE TO SEDUCTION

This work, including images, is protected in all its components by the provisions of the Copyright Law, particularly those relating to copyright. Any reproduction or distribution to third parties, whether free of charge or for a fee, of all or part of this work, is strictly prohibited and constitutes infringement.

Copyright © 2023 – All rights reserved

Aurny AIRDUVAL

Introduction

The concept of the femme fatale has always held a fascination for society. She embodies a captivating blend of charm, mystery, and seduction. The image of the femme fatale is often associated with powerful and irresistible women, capable of turning any man's head. But what lies behind this concept, and how can it be deeply understood? That is what we are going to explore now.

1. The origins of the femme fatale

The concept of the femme fatale has deep roots in history and culture. It has its origins in mythology, literature, and cinema. The term 'femme fatale' is of French origin and literally means 'fatal woman' or 'deadly woman.' It was popularized in the 19th century to describe female characters often portrayed as seductive but dangerous.

One of the earliest notable incarnations of the femme fatale can be found in Greek mythology with figures such as Circe and Medea. These women had the ability to charm and manipulate men at their will, often for personal or malevolent reasons. Their power of seduction was both their asset and their weapon.

Over the centuries, the figure of the femme fatale evolved in literature, notably with iconic characters like Carmen in Bizet's opera or Salome in the Bible. These women were often portrayed as enigmatic, alluring, and seductive figures who drew men towards their tragic destinies.

2. Characteristics of the femme fatale

The femme fatale is a complex character and is often depicted with a number of distinctive characteristics. One of the most obvious characteristics is her power of seduction. She knows how to attract attention and captivate men with her charm, beauty, and confidence.

However, seduction is not her only weapon. The femme fatale is also intelligent and manipulative. She knows how to use her charm to get what she wants, whether it's power, money, or simply admiration. She is often independent and doesn't need to rely on men for her needs.

The femme fatale is also often associated with a certain mystery. Little is known about her past and motivations, which makes her even more intriguing. She can be unpredictable and hard to pin down, which makes her all the more fascinating.

3. The myth of the femme fatale

Is the concept of the femme fatale simply a myth, or can it be a reality that some women aspire to? In reality, the femme fatale is an archetype, a cultural construct that has evolved over time. It is a fictional character that embodies exaggerated qualities to tell captivating stories.

However, this doesn't mean that women can't draw inspiration from certain characteristics of the femme fatale to boost their self-confidence and seductive power. The femme fatale represents a form of female empowerment, where women take control of their own destiny and sexuality.

The femme fatale is a complex and fascinating concept that has captivated the collective imagination for centuries. She embodies seduction, mystery, and power, and she continues to influence today's popular culture. Keep in mind that you can draw inspiration from these characteristics to become a more confident, seductive, and independent woman who can control her own destiny.

Part 1

The foundations of the femme fatale concept

Chapter 1

Myths and realities of the femme fatale

The femme fatale is a powerful concept that has been shaped by culture, literature, and cinema for centuries. She embodies a complex blend of charm, mystery, and seduction. However, behind this concept, many myths and preconceived ideas lurk, deserving exploration. We will demystify the femme fatale by examining the myths that surround her and revealing the realities hidden behind this fascinating figure.

Myth 1: the femme fatale is dangerous and malevolent

One of the most widespread myths about the femme fatale is that she is dangerous and malevolent. She is often portrayed as an unscrupulous manipulator who uses her seduction to bring about the downfall of men. While this image may be true in some works of fiction, it does not reflect reality.

Reality: The femme fatale is a complex and nuanced character. She is not necessarily evil but rather independent and confident. She may use her charm to achieve her goals, but that does not automatically mean she is malevolent. In real life, many attractive women are kind and ethical individuals.

Myth 2: the femme fatale is superficial

Another common myth is that the femme fatale is solely focused on her physical appearance. She is often portrayed as a woman obsessed with her makeup and clothing, willing to do anything to appear seductive.

Reality: The true femme fatale is much more than her appearance. She values self-confidence, intelligence, and effective communication as much as her looks. She knows that seduction is not limited to the exterior but also relies on the interior.

Myth 3: the femme fatale is always independent

Another common stereotype is that the femme fatale is always an independent woman who needs no one. She is often portrayed as a hardened singleton, insensitive to emotions.

Reality: The femme fatale can be independent, but that doesn't mean she never seeks love or relationships. She can have fulfilling relationships while maintaining her independence. The true power of the femme fatale lies in her ability to choose her own path.

Myth 4: the femme fatale has no weaknesses

Some myths suggest that the femme fatale is invulnerable, that she has no weaknesses or emotional vulnerabilities.

Reality: Just like anyone else, the femme fatale can have weaknesses and moments of vulnerability. She can experience failures, doubts, and fears. What sets her apart is her ability to overcome these obstacles with confidence and grace.

Myth 5: the femme fatale is necessarily heterosexual

Another myth to debunk is that the femme fatale is always heterosexual and only seduces men.

Reality: The seduction and charm of the femme fatale are not limited to a single sexual orientation. Femme fatales can be heterosexual, lesbian, bisexual, or of any other orientation. The essence of the femme fatale lies in her self-confidence and her ability to seduce, regardless of her orientation.

Chapter 2

Why becoming a femme fatale can be beneficial

The idea of becoming a femme fatale may raise questions and concerns. Is it a worthwhile goal? Why would you want to cultivate the traits and qualities associated with the femme fatale? We will explore the many reasons why becoming a femme fatale can be beneficial for you, both on a personal level and in your relationships with others.

1. Self-confidence and self-esteem

One of the primary reasons why becoming a femme fatale can be beneficial lies in the enhancement of self-confidence and self-esteem. The femme fatale embodies self-confidence, belief in her abilities, and a positive attitude towards life.

Developing these qualities can have a profound impact on your everyday life. Increased self-confidence enables you to face challenges with assurance, express your opinions convincingly, and pursue your goals with determination. Strong self-esteem helps you love and accept yourself as you are, which is essential for healthy and fulfilling relationships.

2. The power of seduction

Seduction is a subtle art that the femme fatale masters perfectly. Learning to seduce effectively is not just about romantic relationships but also about how you interact with others in all aspects of your life. Seduction involves capturing people's attention, making them feel special, and creating meaningful connections.

When you master this art, you become more influential and capable of generating enthusiasm in others for your ideas and goals. You can forge fruitful professional relationships, build strong networks, and inspire confidence in all your interactions.

3. Independence and autonomy

The femme fatale is often portrayed as an independent woman who relies on no one to achieve her goals. This independence is a valuable quality to cultivate. It means that you have the power to make informed decisions, follow your own path, and not be constrained by the expectations or opinions of others.

Independence allows you to pursue your dreams and passions without hindrance. It also gives you the ability to create a life that fully satisfies you, whether you are single or in a relationship.

4. Achieving Professional Success

In the professional world, qualities associated with the femme fatale, such as self-confidence, seduction, and independence, can be valuable assets. Femme fatales are often perceived as natural leaders, capable of making informed decisions and leading with charisma.

These qualities can help you advance in your career, seize opportunities, and gain the recognition you deserve. They also assist you in successfully navigating complex professional situations, such as negotiations and team management.

5. Fulfilling relationships

The traits of the femme fatale can also enhance your personal and romantic relationships. Effective communication, strong self-confidence, and well-developed seductive power are key elements in building deep and meaningful connections with others.

You can create fulfilling romantic relationships based on mutual respect, passion, and understanding. You can also forge strong and lasting friendships by using these skills to establish authentic connections with others.

Part 2

Self-confidence and self-esteem

Chapter 3

The importance of self-confidence

Self-confidence is one of the most fundamental qualities for becoming a femme fatale. It is the cornerstone upon which many other characteristics associated with this image rest. We will delve into the importance of self-confidence and how it can help you become a more accomplished femme fatale.

1. What is self-confidence ?

Self-confidence is a feeling of faith and conviction in your own abilities, decisions, and worth as an individual. It is the belief in your ability to meet challenges, achieve your goals, and confront obstacles with determination.

Self-confidence is not limited to a single dimension of your life. It encompasses all aspects of your being, including your self-esteem, personal assurance, and your ability to interact with others positively.

2. The benefits of self-confidence

Self-confidence brings many benefits that can significantly enhance your life. Here are some of the key benefits of self-confidence:

Personal success: Self-confidence is often a determining factor in personal success. When you believe in your skills and your ability to achieve your goals, you are more likely to accomplish them.

Effective communication: Self-confidence facilitates communication. You can express your thoughts and ideas clearly and convincingly, which helps you influence others positively.

Self-esteem: Self-confidence contributes to strong self-esteem. You appreciate and respect yourself more, which enhances your emotional well-being.

Resilience: When you have self-confidence, you are better prepared to face setbacks and challenges. You have the resilience to bounce back from failures.

Seduction: Self-confidence is a key element of seduction. When you are confident in your own allure, it is reflected in your attitude and behavior.

Taking calculated risks: You are more inclined to take calculated risks when you have self-confidence. This can lead you to seize opportunities you might not have considered otherwise.

3. Building self-confidence

Self-confidence is not an innate quality but rather a skill that can be developed and strengthened over time. Here are some strategies for cultivating self-confidence:

Self-awareness: Understanding your strengths and weaknesses is essential for building self-confidence. Take the time to know yourself and accept all aspects of your being.

Goal-setting: Establishing realistic and attainable goals allows you to measure your success and enhance your self-confidence as you achieve them.

Positive thinking: Avoid self-destructive and negative thoughts. Replace them with positive and encouraging affirmations.

Acceptance of failure: Understand that failure is a natural part of life. Instead of fearing it, use it as an opportunity for learning and growth.

Communication practice: Improve your communication skills by practicing regularly. This can include public speaking, interpersonal communication, and conflict resolution.

Stress management: Learn to manage stress and anxiety, as they can impede your self-confidence. Meditation, deep breathing, and physical exercise are excellent strategies to achieve this.

4. Self-confidence and the femme fatale

The femme fatale embodies self-confidence brilliantly. She knows she is desirable and powerful, and this assurance shines through in her attitude. She can captivate others because she believes in her own seduction.

When you develop self-confidence, you become more capable of embodying the traits of the femme fatale. You can seduce with conviction, make informed decisions, and navigate confidently in all situations. Your self-confidence is the foundation upon which your transformation into a fulfilled and accomplished femme fatale rests.

Chapter 4

Building strong self-esteem

Self-esteem is a crucial element of self-confidence and the femme fatale image. Strong self-esteem allows you to love and respect yourself, which is essential for becoming a confident and seductive woman. We will explore the importance of self-esteem and how you can cultivate it to reach your full potential as a femme fatale.

1. What is self-esteem?

Self-esteem is the value you place on yourself as an individual. It encompasses your beliefs, perceptions, and emotions about yourself. When you have strong self-esteem, you have a positive and realistic opinion of yourself, which allows you to love and accept yourself as you are.

It is important to note that self-esteem is not synonymous with arrogance or narcissism. It is based on a balanced understanding of your strengths and weaknesses, as well as self-acceptance as an imperfect human being.

2. Signs of strong self-esteem

How do you know if you have strong self-esteem? Here are some signs that indicate your self-esteem is healthy:

Self-confidence: You believe in your abilities and have confidence in your potential for success.

Resilience: You can face setbacks and failures without questioning your self-worth.

Self-love: You love and respect yourself, regardless of your imperfections.

Assertiveness: You can express your needs, opinions, and boundaries assertively.

Independence: You have a sense of independence and personal responsibility.

Ability to handle criticism: You can manage constructive criticism without feeling personally attacked.

3. The importance of self-esteem for the femme fatale

Self-esteem is particularly important for the femme fatale. Here's how it plays an essential role in achieving the image of the femme fatale:

Confidence in her allure: Strong self-esteem allows you to believe in your power of seduction. You don't need constant approval from others to feel alluring.

Emotional independence: Strong self-esteem makes you less reliant on the approval of others. You can forge your own path and make decisions based on your personal needs and values.

Relationship management: Self-esteem helps you establish healthy and balanced relationships. You don't tolerate toxic or abusive relationships because you know you deserve better.

Emotional resilience: You can overcome rejections and disappointments without questioning your own worth. This enables you to continue seeking relationships and opportunities that suit you better.

4. Developing strong self-esteem

Developing strong self-esteem is an ongoing process that requires time and effort. Here are some strategies to develop and strengthen your self-esteem:

Self-compassion: Treat yourself with kindness and compassion, as you would for a friend. Be gentle with yourself, even when you make mistakes.

Self-acceptance: Embrace your imperfections and weaknesses. Nobody is perfect, and that's what makes us unique.

Setting realistic goals: Establish realistic and achievable goals. Celebrate your successes, no matter their magnitude.

Learning from failure: Understand that failure is a natural part of life. Use it as an opportunity for learning and growth.

Assertive communication: Learn to express your needs, opinions, and boundaries assertively, without apologizing for who you are.

Seeking support: If you have difficulty cultivating strong self-esteem, consider consulting a mental health professional. Therapy can be a valuable tool for enhancing your self-esteem.

Chapter 5

Developing a positive attitude

The attitude you adopt towards life and towards yourself plays a crucial role in your ability to become a confident and alluring femme fatale. A positive attitude can boost your self-confidence, enhance your emotional well-being, and help you achieve your goals. We will explore the importance of a positive attitude and how you can develop it to enrich your life.

1. What is a positive attitude ?

A positive attitude is a way of viewing the world that emphasizes the positive and constructive aspects of life. It means adopting an optimistic perspective, even in the face of challenges and setbacks. A positive attitude is characterized by gratitude, resilience, optimism, and self-confidence.

2. The benefits of a positive attitude

Developing a positive attitude brings numerous advantages that are particularly relevant for becoming an accomplished femme fatale:

Enhanced self-confidence: A positive attitude helps you believe in your abilities and maintain strong self-confidence, even when facing obstacles.

Seduction and charisma: A positive attitude is magnetic. It attracts others and makes you more alluring by creating a light and pleasant atmosphere around you.

Emotional resilience: A positive attitude helps you face setbacks with calm and determination. You are better prepared to overcome challenges.

Emotional well-being: A positive attitude is linked to improved emotional well-being. You are happier, less stressed, and more satisfied with your life.

Optimism for the future: A positive attitude allows you to view the future with optimism, encouraging you to pursue your goals with passion and determination.

3. Strategies to develop a positive attitude

Developing a positive attitude is a process that requires practice and perseverance. Here are some strategies to help you cultivate a positive attitude:

Gratitude: Make it a habit to jot down things you're grateful for each day. This helps you focus on the positive aspects of your life.

Realistic optimism: Cultivate realistic optimism by believing in your ability to overcome challenges while remaining aware of realities.

Avoiding negativity: Steer clear of negative individuals and toxic influences. Surround yourself with people who support and inspire you.

Positive visualization: Visualize your goals and dreams positively. Picture yourself succeeding and feeling satisfaction.

Meditation and mindfulness: Meditation and mindfulness can help you stay grounded in the present moment, reduce stress, and cultivate a positive attitude.

Positive affirmations: Use positive affirmations to boost your self-confidence and maintain an optimistic outlook.

Finding meaning: Find meaning in what you do. When you have a meaningful purpose, it's easier to maintain a positive attitude.

4. The positive attitude and the femme fatale image

Positive attitude is a key element of the femme fatale image. It embodies seduction, self-confidence, and optimism. Here's how a positive attitude plays a central role in achieving the femme fatale image:

Radiant seduction: A positive attitude makes you radiant and draws others in. Your zest for life and natural charm are seductive assets.

Dazzling self-confidence: A positive attitude enhances your self-confidence, allowing you to seduce with conviction and assurance.

Seductive resilience: A positive attitude makes you resilient in the face of rejection and romantic challenges. You can maintain an optimistic outlook and continue seeking love.

Magnetic attraction: Positive individuals generally attract positive partners and friends. Your attitude can help you create fulfilling relationships.

Part 3

The power of seduction

Chapter 6

The fundamentals of seduction

Seduction is one of the most emblematic aspects of the femme fatale image. It involves captivating the attention of others, creating a deep connection, and sparking enthusiasm. We will explore the fundamentals of seduction and how you can develop this skill to become an irresistible femme fatale.

1. Understanding seduction

Seduction is a subtle art that relies on communication, self-confidence, and an understanding of the desires and motivations of others. It is not limited to physical attraction but also encompasses intellectual and emotional seduction.

Seduction involves creating an atmosphere of charm and mystery that draws others toward you. It's a way of presenting yourself irresistibly, sparking interest, and establishing a deep connection.

2. Key elements of seduction

To become an alluring femme fatale, it is essential to master the key elements of seduction:

Self-confidence: Self-confidence is one of the pillars of seduction. When you believe in your own allure, it shows in your attitude and behavior.

Communication: Effective communication is crucial for establishing a connection. Actively listen to others, ask questions, and show a genuine interest in what they're saying.

Body language: Your body language plays a crucial role in seduction. Maintain eye contact, adopt an open posture, and use subtle gestures to express your interest.

Charisma: Charisma is the ability to draw others to you with your magnetic presence. It is built on confidence, positivity, and warmth.

Mystery: Mystery is a key element of seduction. Don't reveal everything about yourself immediately. Let others gradually discover your personality.

Sense of humor: Humor is a powerful tool of seduction. A well-developed sense of humor can create a light and pleasant atmosphere.

3. Seduction in romantic relationships

In the context of romantic relationships, seduction plays an essential role in creating a deep and passionate connection. Here's how you can apply the principles of seduction to your love life:

Create anticipation: Seduction involves building anticipation and desire. Don't hesitate to play with mystery and maintain a certain level of restraint.

Express your interest: Show your interest in the other person subtly. A smile, prolonged eye contact, and sincere compliments can work wonders.

Actively listen: Seduction isn't just about talking about yourself. Listen carefully to what the other person is saying and show that you care about their thoughts and feelings.

Create special moments: Plan special moments that allow you to connect on a deeper level. Romantic dinners, getaways, and thoughtful gestures are ways to enhance seduction.

Be authentic: While seduction may include some performance, it's essential to remain authentic. Don't pretend to be someone you're not.

4. Seduction in everyday life

Seduction is not limited to romantic relationships. It can also be applied in your daily life to positively influence others and create meaningful connections. Here's how to use seduction in different contexts:

Professional seduction: Use seduction to build fruitful professional relationships. Be charismatic, express your self-confidence, and show genuine interest in others in a professional setting.

Social seduction: In social situations, showcase your charm and sense of humor. Be a pleasant person to be around and create authentic connections.

Personal seduction: Apply the principles of seduction to strengthen your personal relationships. Listen carefully to your friends and family, show them that you care, and create a positive atmosphere.

Chapter 7

Seductive body language

Body language plays an essential role in seduction. It can be even more powerful than the words you speak. We will explore the significance of seductive body language and how you can use it to become an irresistible femme fatale.

1. The importance of body language

Body language is how you communicate with your body, gestures, posture, and facial expressions. It can reveal a lot about your emotions, intentions, and your level of self-confidence. When used in a seductive manner, it can create a deep connection with others

2. Key elements of seductive body language

To develop seductive body language, it's essential to master some key elements:

Eye contact: Eye contact is one of the most powerful aspects of seductive body language. It shows that you are attentive to the other person and confident in yourself.

Smile: A warm and genuine smile can establish an instant connection. It demonstrates that you are open, friendly, and happy to be in the other person's presence.

Posture: Maintaining an upright and open posture is important for seduction. It shows that you are confident and open to interaction.

Subtle gestures: Use subtle gestures to express your interest. For example, tilt your head slightly when listening, gently touch the other person's arm to emphasize an important point, or play with your hair casually.

Graceful movements: Fluid and graceful movements add to your allure. Avoid abrupt or awkward gestures.

Physical closeness: When comfortable, move slightly closer to the other person to create a sense of intimacy.

Avoid barriers: Avoid crossing your arms or legs, as it can signal a defensive attitude. Keep your body open.

3. Body language in romantic relationships

In romantic relationships, body language is particularly important for creating a passionate connection. Here's how you can use body language to enhance your seduction:

Intense eye contact: Intense eye contact can create sexual tension. Gaze deeply into your partner's eyes in a sensual manner.

Gentle touch: Gentle touches, such as soft caresses, light kisses, and cuddling, enhance physical intimacy.

Closeness: When you're with your partner, maintain subtle physical closeness to create an intimate atmosphere.

Provocative posture: Adopt a posture that highlights your physical assets while remaining elegant and graceful.

Anticipation: Use suggestive gestures to build anticipation. For example, run your fingers suggestively over your lower lip.

4. Body language in everyday life

Body language isn't limited to romantic moments. You can also use it in your daily life to positively influence others and create authentic connections. Here's how to use body language in different contexts:

Professional seduction: Use confident and open body language to create a magnetic presence at work. Eye contact, posture, and a smile can help you build successful professional relationships.

Social seduction: In social situations, adopt a warm and open attitude. Your body language can help you create authentic connections with others.

Personal seduction: Use body language to strengthen your personal relationships. A genuine smile, eye contact, and friendly gestures show that you care about others.

Chapter 8

Effective communication

Communication is the primary tool of seduction and influence. Effective communication can help you create deep connections, express your needs and desires, and positively influence others. We will explore the importance of effective communication and how you can develop this skill to become a successful femme fatale.

1. The importance of effective communication

Communication is the means by which you interact with the world around you. It encompasses not only the words you speak but also your body language, tone of voice, and facial expressions. Effective communication is essential for building meaningful relationships and positively influencing others.

2. Key elements of effective communication

To develop effective communication, it's essential to master certain key elements:

Active listening: Active listening involves giving your full attention to what the other person is saying. Listen not only to the words but also to the underlying emotions and intentions.

Clear expression: Express your thoughts and feelings in a clear and concise manner. Avoid ambiguity and confusing messages.

Body language: Your body language also communicates important information. Maintain an open posture, sustain eye contact, and use subtle gestures to complement your words.

Tone of voice: Your tone of voice can convey emotions. Speak with a warm and engaging tone to create a positive connection.

Asking questions: Ask questions to show your interest in the other person and to deepen the conversation.

Empathy: Try to understand the other person's emotions and perspectives. Show empathy and understanding.

Clarity in objectives: Clearly define your communication objectives. What do you want to achieve with this interaction?

3. Communication in relationships

In romantic relationships, effective communication is essential for creating a deep and passionate connection. Here's how you can apply the principles of effective communication in your love life:

Active listening: Listen attentively to your partner to understand their needs, desires, and concerns. Show empathy and be open to their emotions.

Expressing your feelings: Share your feelings honestly and openly. Discuss your joys, concerns, and desires with your partner.

Conflict resolution: Use communication skills to resolve conflicts constructively. Avoid accusations and criticism and focus on finding solutions.

Building emotional intimacy: Open and honest communication contributes to building deep emotional intimacy with your partner.

4. Communication in everyday life

Effective communication is useful in all aspects of everyday life, whether at work, in social situations, or in personal relationships. Here's how to use effective communication in different contexts:

Professional seduction: Use communication to build fruitful professional relationships. Be clear in your messages, actively listen to your colleagues, and collaborate effectively.

Social seduction: In social situations, be a pleasant person to be around by using positive body language and engaging communication.

Personal seduction: Use communication to strengthen your personal relationships. Express your love and appreciation to your friends and family, and resolve conflicts constructively.

Part 4

The art of conversation

Chapter 9

A captivating conversation

A captivating conversation is one of the most powerful ways to establish deep connections with others and ignite enthusiasm. It can help you become a confident femme fatale by drawing attention and creating meaningful relationships. We will explore the art of captivating conversation and how you can develop this skill.

1. The art of captivating conversation

Captivating conversation goes beyond mere words. It involves the art of creating engaging and enriching interactions that leave a lasting impression. Here are some key elements of captivating conversation:

Active listening: Genuine conversation starts with active listening. Pay close attention to what the other person is saying, without interrupting or preparing your response.

Ask open-ended questions: Ask open-ended questions that encourage the other person to express themselves in detail. Avoid closed questions that require short answers.

Share stories: Personal stories are a powerful way to build a connection. Share anecdotes from your life that are relevant to the conversation.

Show interest: Display genuine interest in what the other person is saying. Ask follow-up questions to deepen the discussion.

Express emotions: Don't be afraid to express your emotions authentically. This allows the other person to emotionally connect with you.

Smile and eye contact: Use a warm smile and maintain eye contact to show your engagement in the conversation.

Avoid interruptions: Refrain from cutting off the other person. Let them speak and wait for your turn to talk.

2. Conversation in romantic relationships

In romantic relationships, engaging conversation is essential to maintain a deep and passionate connection. Here's how you can apply the principles of captivating conversation in your love life:

Deep listening: Listen attentively to your partner, paying special attention to their thoughts, feelings, and needs. Show empathy and understanding.

Intimate sharing: Share intimate moments from your life and emotions. This strengthens the emotional connection with your partner.

Playful conversation: Introduce playful elements into your conversations to maintain excitement and lightness in the relationship.

Express your desires: Be open to discussing your desires and needs with your partner. Honest communication is essential for maintaining a fulfilling relationship.

3. Conversation in everyday life

Captivating conversation can also be used in your everyday life to positively influence others and create meaningful connections. Here's how you can use captivating conversation in different contexts:

Professional Seduction: In a professional context, engage in captivating conversations to establish fruitful relationships. Show interest in your colleagues and collaborate effectively.

Social Seduction: In social situations, engage in interesting conversations by asking open-ended questions and sharing personal stories. Create authentic connections with others.

Personal Seduction: Use captivating conversation to strengthen your personal relationships. Express your love and appreciation for your friends and family, and engage in meaningful discussions.

Chapter 10

Humor and charm

Humor and charm are powerful assets for becoming an alluring and irresistible femme fatale. Humor can lighten a conversation, create a pleasant atmosphere, and spark enthusiasm, while charm can make you magnetic and captivating. We will explore the importance of humor and charm and how to develop them to enrich your femme fatale personality.

1. Humor: the power of making people laugh

Humor is one of the most effective ways to connect with others. It can brighten up a conversation, relieve tension, and make you more approachable. Here's how to use humor in a charming way:

Sense of humor: Develop a sense of humor that suits your personality. Humor can be subtle, sarcastic, ironic, or even absurd, depending on your preferences.

Self-deprecation: Self-deprecation means light-heartedly making fun of yourself without being critical. It shows that you are comfortable with yourself.

Humor in situations: Use humor appropriately in different situations. It can be used to ease tension in stressful moments or to add some lightheartedness to a conversation.

Listening to others: Pay attention to how others react when you make a joke. If someone feels uncomfortable, be prepared to clarify or apologize.

Shared humor: Shared humor creates a special connection. Try to find common humorous topics with others.

2. Charm: the art of captivating

Charm is the art of captivating others with your magnetic presence. It relies on confidence, positivity, and a warm attitude. Here's how to develop your charm:

Self-confidence: Self-confidence is the foundation of charm. Believe in yourself and your ability to enchant others.

Warm smile: A warm smile is a powerful tool for charm. It shows that you are open, friendly, and happy to be in the company of others.

Eye contact: Maintain confident and engaging eye contact. It demonstrates that you are attentive and interested in the person in front of you.

Active listening: Active listening is essential to show that you care about others. Listen attentively to what they say and ask questions to deepen the conversation.

Mystery: Mystery can be charming. Don't reveal everything about yourself immediately. Let others gradually discover your personality.

3. Humor and charm in romantic relationships

In romantic relationships, humor and charm play an essential role in maintaining a passionate connection. Here's how to use them in your love life:

Humor in the relationship: Share funny moments with your partner to create positive memories. Laughing together strengthens the bond and fosters a sense of camaraderie.

Romantic charm: Use charm to create special romantic moments. Candlelit dinners, surprise evenings, and thoughtful gestures are all ways to maintain charm in the relationship.

4. Humor and charm in everyday life

Humor and charm are not limited to romantic moments. You can also apply them in your everyday life to positively influence others and create authentic connections. Here's how to apply them in various contexts:

Professional charm: Use humor and charm to establish fruitful professional relationships. Be a pleasant presence in the workplace.

Social charm: In social situations, add a touch of humor to conversations. Be charming by showing genuine interest in others.

Personal charm: Use humor and charm to strengthen your personal relationships. Create fun moments with friends and family and be a charming presence.

Chapter 11

Seductive topics of conversation

Knowing how to choose the right conversation topics is essential to become a seductive femme fatale. The topics you bring up can positively influence how others perceive you and create deep connections. We'll explore seductive conversation topics and how to use them to enhance your interactions.

1. The art of choosing topics for conversation

Choosing the right conversation topics is a blend of art and understanding your conversation partner. It involves finding common ground, sparking interest, and creating a connection. Here are some principles to keep in mind:

Know your audience: Understanding the interests and concerns of the person you're talking to is essential. Listen carefully to identify topics that excite them.

Diversify topics: Avoid sticking to a single type of subject. Vary conversation themes to maintain interest.

Ask open-ended questions: Pose open-ended questions that encourage the other person to express themselves in detail. Avoid closed-ended questions that elicit short responses.

Share experiences: Share personal experiences and relevant anecdotes to make the conversation more lively and personal.

Current events: Current events can be an endless source of conversation. Keep an eye on the news and recent happenings to fuel your discussions.

2. Examples of attractive conversation topics

Seductive conversation topics are those that stimulate interest, evoke enthusiasm, and enhance your charm. Here are some examples of seductive conversation topics:

Travel: Travel is often an exciting topic. Discuss the destinations you've visited, the experiences you've had, and the places you dream of exploring.

Film and culture: Talk about the latest movies, captivating books you've read, or art exhibitions you've visited.

Passions and hobbies: Share your passions and hobbies. What do you do for fun and relaxation? Share your experiences and plans.

Health and well-being: Topics related to health, fitness, and well-being are important. Discuss your eating habits, exercise routine, or tips for staying in shape.

Projects and goals: Discuss your future projects and goals. What are your dreams and aspirations? Share them with enthusiasm.

Cultural events: Talk about upcoming cultural events, such as concerts, exhibitions, festivals, or plays you plan to attend.

Personal development: Topics related to personal development, such as meditation, personal growth, or self-help books, can be inspiring.

3. Conversation in romantic relationships

In romantic relationships, choosing conversation topics can deepen the connection and maintain passion. Here's how to use them in your love life:

Sharing emotions: Express your emotions and feelings honestly. Talk about your expectations, desires, and concerns.

Planning together: Discuss your future plans as a couple. Talk about common dreams and how you can achieve them together.

4. Conversations in everyday life

In your everyday life, captivating conversation topics can help you positively influence others and build genuine connections. Here's how to apply them in different contexts:

Professional seduction: In professional conversations, discuss topics relevant to your field. Share your ideas and projects with enthusiasm.

Social seduction: In social situations, be open to discussing a variety of subjects to create authentic connections with others.

Personal seduction: Use captivating conversation topics to strengthen your personal relationships. Actively listen to your friends and family and share meaningful moments with them.

Part 5

Appearance and style

Chapter 12

Taking care of your physical appearance

Physical appearance plays an important role in seduction and creating a memorable impression. Taking care of your physical appearance can boost your self-confidence, attract attention, and contribute to becoming an attractive and irresistible femme fatale. We will explore the significance of tending to your physical appearance and provide you with tips to enhance your look.

1. The importance of physical appearance

Physical appearance is the first thing others notice when you enter a room. It sends an instant message about who you are and how you feel about yourself. Here's why physical appearance is important:

Self-confidence: Taking care of your appearance can boost your self-confidence. When you feel good in your skin, it reflects in your attitude and behavior.

Attracting attention: A well-groomed appearance naturally attracts attention. People are more inclined to be interested in you and want to get to know you.

Creating a positive first impression: The first impression is often the most memorable. A well-groomed appearance can create a positive first impression that opens doors in all areas of your life.

2. Tips for looking after your physical appearance

Here are some tips for taking care of your physical appearance in a seductive manner:

Clothing: Choose outfits that flatter you and align with your personal style. Opt for clothing that makes you feel comfortable and confident.

Personal hygiene: Maintain good personal hygiene by taking regular showers, brushing your teeth, caring for your hair, and using skincare products suitable for your skin type.

Skincare: Take care of your skin by using quality products to cleanse and moisturize your face. Healthy and radiant skin is an attractive asset.

Makeup (if you wear it): If you use makeup, go for a natural look that enhances your features without overdoing it. The goal is to appear naturally beautiful.

Hairstyle: Choose a hairstyle that suits you and reflects your personality. Regular appointments with a hairstylist can help keep your haircut in good shape.

Accessories: Accessories can add an elegant touch to your look. Select jewelry, handbags, and shoes that complement your outfit.

Diet and exercise: A balanced diet and regular physical activity contribute to a healthy physical appearance and help you feel good in your body.

Posture: Maintain a confident and upright posture. Good posture can instantly make you appear more seductive.

3. Physical appearance in romantic relationships

In romantic relationships, physical appearance continues to play a significant role. Here's how to optimize it in your love life:

Personal seduction: Take care of your appearance to show your partner that you care about being attractive. This can help maintain passion in the relationship.

Self-confidence: A well-groomed appearance can boost your self-confidence, which is attractive to your partner.

4. Physical appearance in everyday life

In your daily life, physical appearance can positively influence others and create authentic connections. Here's how to use it in different contexts:

Professional seduction: A well-groomed professional appearance is essential for success at work. Choose appropriate attire for your industry and maintain impeccable personal hygiene.

Social seduction: In social situations, take care of your appearance to demonstrate your respect for others and your appreciation of their company.

Chapter 13

The femme fatale style of dress

Clothing style is a key element in the physical appearance of a femme fatale. It allows you to express yourself, enhance your personality and create a memorable impression. Let's take a look at the femme fatale's style of dress, focusing on clothing choices, accessories and tips for creating a seductive and elegant look.

1. The importance of clothing style

Clothing style is a powerful means of communicating who you are and what you represent. It can reflect your self-confidence, creativity, and attention to detail. Here's why clothing style is important:

Expression of personality: Your clothing style is a form of expressing your personality. It allows you to show the world who you are.

Self-confidence: Wearing clothes that make you feel comfortable in your own skin boosts your self-confidence. This is reflected in your demeanor.

Creating a memorable impression: Your clothing style can help you make a lasting first impression, whether in social or professional situations

2. The femme fatale's clothing style

The femme fatale's clothing style is characterized by its elegance, self-confidence, and subtle sex appeal. Here are some key elements of the femme fatale's clothing style:

Self-confidence: Self-confidence is the foundation of the femme fatale's clothing style. Wear clothes that make you feel powerful and irresistible.

Elegant outfits: Opt for stylish and well-fitting outfits that accentuate your assets. Dresses, suits, and coordinated ensembles are common choices.

Colors: Choose colors that complement you and match your complexion. Classic colors like black, white, red, and navy blue are often associated with the femme fatale style.

Accessories: Accessories can add a touch of elegance to your look. Opt for discreet jewelry and quality handbags to complete your outfit.

Footwear: Shoes are a crucial element of the femme fatale style. Well-maintained high heels can elongate your legs and improve your posture.

Balance: Balance sensuality with sophistication. You can show some skin subtly, but avoid overly provocative outfits.

3. Tips for creating a seductive clothing style

Here are some tips to create a seductive clothing style for a femme fatale:

Find your signature: Identify a unique style element, whether it's a color, a clothing cut, or an accessory. This can become your signature.

Invest in quality: Opt for quality clothing that will last over time. Quality is visible and tangible.

Adapt to the occasion: Adjust your style according to the occasion. You can be elegant at work, sexy in the evening, and casual on the weekend.

Be comfortable: Wear clothing in which you feel comfortable and confident. Comfort is essential to exude a seductive aura.

Seek inspiration: Find inspiration in fashion magazines, on social media, or by observing women with styles that attract you.

4. Clothing style in romantic relationships

In romantic relationships, clothing style can contribute to maintaining attraction and creating a passionate connection. Here's how to optimize it in your love life:

Variety: Change your outfits from time to time to maintain excitement. Surprise your partner by wearing different looks.

Romance: For romantic moments, choose outfits that enhance your sensuality while remaining elegant.

5. Clothing style in everyday life

In your daily life, your clothing style can positively influence others and create authentic connections. Here's how to use it in different contexts:

Professional Seduction: Wear professional outfits that reflect your seriousness and competence. Dressing elegantly at work helps create a positive impression.

Social Seduction: In social situations, adapt your style according to the occasion. Show respect for others by presenting yourself appropriately.

Chapter 14

The secrets of timeless beauty

Timeless beauty is a valuable asset in becoming a seductive and irresistible femme fatale. Unlike fleeting beauty, timeless beauty is based on self-care habits and an attitude that withstands the test of time. We will explore the secrets of timeless beauty, focusing on skincare, mental health, and tips to maintain your radiance through the years.

1. Definition of timeless beauty

Timeless beauty is a beauty that transcends the ages. It depends not only on physical appearance but also on self-confidence, mental health, and overall well-being. Here are the characteristics of timeless beauty:

Self-confidence: Self-confidence is an essential component of timeless beauty. A person who feels comfortable in their own skin exudes a magnetic aura.

Mental health: Mental health is a key factor in timeless beauty. Serenity, positivity, and the ability to manage stress contribute to a radiant appearance.

Skin care: Taking care of your skin is an important habit to maintain timeless beauty. Healthy, well-moisturized skin ages more gracefully.

Hydration and nutrition: Drinking enough water and maintaining a balanced diet contribute to timeless beauty by nourishing the body from the inside.

2. Secrets of timeless beauty

Here are some secrets to cultivate timeless beauty over the years:

Skin care: Establish a skincare routine tailored to your skin type. Cleanse, moisturize, and protect your skin from the sun to prevent premature aging.

Balanced diet: Consume a diet rich in fruits, vegetables, lean proteins, and whole grains. Antioxidants and essential nutrients nourish your skin and hair.

Hydration: Drink enough water to keep your skin well-hydrated. Water helps eliminate toxins and maintain skin elasticity.

Exercise: Regular exercise promotes blood circulation, delivering essential nutrients to the skin and muscles. It also contributes to stress management.

Sleep: Sleep is essential for cellular regeneration. Ensure you get enough sleep every night for your skin to repair itself.

Stress management: Practice stress management techniques like meditation, deep breathing, or yoga. Stress can contribute to premature aging.

Self-confidence: Work on your self-confidence by surrounding yourself with positive people, setting goals, and celebrating your successes.

Positivity: Cultivate a positive attitude through practicing gratitude and avoiding negativity. A positive attitude radiates and attracts others.

3. Timeless beauty in romantic relationships

In romantic relationships, timeless beauty can help maintain attraction and create a passionate connection. Here's how to optimize it in your love life:

Self-confidence: Self-confidence is particularly attractive in a relationship. It allows you to express your love and maintain passion.

Mental health: Balanced mental health promotes harmonious relationships. The ability to manage stress and emotions strengthens emotional stability in the relationship.

4. Timeless beauty in everyday life

In your daily life, timeless beauty can positively influence others and create authentic connections. Here's how to use it in different contexts:

Professional seduction: Self-confidence and stress management are valuable assets at work. They help you handle professional challenges with grace.

Social seduction: In social situations, a positive attitude and beautiful energy attract others. Be a radiant presence.

Part 6

The management of relationships

Chapter 15

Building healthy relationships

Interpersonal relationships play a crucial role in the life of a femme fatale. Healthy and positive relationships contribute to her personal growth and her ability to seduce authentically. We will explore the importance of establishing healthy relationships, whether in the realm of romance, work, or social interactions, and provide you with tips for nurturing positive relationships.

1. The importance of healthy relationships

The importance of healthy relationships is significant for several reasons:

Personal growth: Healthy relationships contribute to your personal growth. They provide emotional support, attentive listening, and opportunities for personal development.

Self-confidence: Positive relationships strengthen your self-confidence. They demonstrate that you are appreciated and valued by others.

Emotional well-being: Healthy relationships promote emotional well-being. They reduce stress and bring joy and happiness into your life.

Social network: Healthy relationships expand your social network, which can be beneficial both professionally and personally

2. Tips for building healthy relationships

Here are some tips for establishing and maintaining healthy relationships in various areas of your life:

a. In romantic relationships

Communication: open and honest communication is the key to a healthy romantic relationship. Express your needs, desires, and concerns respectfully.

Respect: mutual respect is essential. Respect each other's boundaries and expect the same in return.

Emotional support: be there for each other when needed. Offer emotional support when your partner is going through tough times.

Sharing: spend quality time together. Foster emotional intimacy by sharing your dreams, plans, and experiences.

b. In professional relationships

Collaboration: Foster collaboration and communication within your team. Work together to achieve your professional goals.

Respect: Respect the opinions and skills of your colleagues. Avoid unnecessary conflicts and prioritize constructive problem-solving.

Positive Leadership: If you hold a leadership position, exhibit positive leadership by encouraging the growth and development of your team.

Networking: Build a professional network by participating in events, connecting with colleagues, and seeking mentorship opportunities.

C. In social relationships

Active listening: Be an attentive listener when you talk to your friends and family. Show interest in their concerns and successes.

Empathy: Show empathy towards others. Try to understand their emotions and support them in difficult times.

Sharing: Share positive experiences with your friends and family. Create memories together by doing activities you enjoy.

Balance: Maintain a balance between your social life and other commitments. Take time to relax and have fun with your loved ones.

d. Managing toxic relationships

It's important to recognize and manage toxic relationships. If a relationship is causing you stress, anxiety, or emotional suffering, consider taking steps to either preserve it or end it if necessary.

Assessment: Evaluate the relationship objectively. Examine how it affects you emotionally, mentally, and physically.

Communication: Try to communicate your concerns with the person involved. Sometimes, an honest discussion can resolve issues.

Boundaries: Set clear boundaries to protect your emotional well-being. If the relationship doesn't improve, consider distancing yourself.

Chapter 16

Seduction in an existing relationship

Seduction is not limited to the beginnings of a relationship. It continues to play a role in maintaining passion, intimacy, and emotional connection in an existing relationship. We will explore how to sustain and rekindle seduction in a long-term relationship, whether it's in a romantic relationship or a lasting partnership.

1. The importance of ongoing seduction

Continuous seduction is crucial for nourishing and strengthening an existing relationship. Here's why it is so important:

Passion: Seduction maintains passion and excitement in the relationship, preventing routine from setting in.

Intimacy: It promotes emotional and physical intimacy, thus strengthening the connection between partners.

Confidence: Continuous seduction boosts self-confidence and confidence in the relationship because it demonstrates that the attraction persists.

Renewal: It allows for the renewal of the relationship, discovering new aspects of your partner and maintaining commitment.

2. The keys to ongoing seduction

Here are some keys to maintaining seduction in an existing relationship:

Open communication: Honest and open communication is essential. Discuss your desires, fantasies, and expectations to maintain emotional connection.

Dates and special moments: Plan regular dates or special moments together. It can be as simple as a movie night at home or a romantic getaway.

Surprise your partner: Surprise your partner from time to time with romantic gestures, small gifts, or unexpected sweet words.

Sexual exploration: Explore new sexual experiences together to keep the passion alive. Be open to experimentation and communication during intimacy.

Appreciate the little moments: Don't forget to appreciate the small moments of daily connection, like a morning hug or a goodnight kiss.

Maintain your identity: Continue working on your personal development and cultivate your individual passions. A fulfilled person is more attractive.

3. Seduction in a romantic relationship

In a romantic relationship, ongoing seduction is particularly important. Here are some specific tips:

Empathetic listening: Listen carefully to your partner, show empathy, and respond to their emotional needs.

Romance: Romance should not disappear over time. Plan romantic dinners, getaways, and surprises for your partner.

Express your feelings: Don't forget to tell your partner how much you love them and how much they mean to you.

4. Seduction in a long-term partnership

In a long-term partnership, ongoing seduction is just as important to maintain connection and satisfaction. Here are specific tips:

Communication: Open communication is crucial for resolving issues and conflicts constructively.

Shared responsibilities: Share responsibilities in the relationship in a balanced way to avoid overwork and stress.

Maintain emotional intimacy: Preserve emotional intimacy by sharing your thoughts, dreams, and concerns.

5. Seduction in everyday life

Seduction in everyday life should not be overlooked. It can positively influence others and create authentic connections. Here's how to use it in different contexts:

Professional seduction: Professional seduction involves demonstrating your competence, self-confidence, and integrity at work. Be a positive leader and a source of inspiration for your colleagues.

Social seduction: In social situations, show interest in others, maintain a positive attitude, and engage in enriching conversations.

Chapter 17

Managing relationship challenges

Relationship challenges are an integral part of any relationship, whether it's romantic, friendly, familial, or professional. Knowing how to address these challenges constructively is essential for maintaining healthy and fulfilling relationships. We will explore common relationship challenges and provide you with advice on how to manage them successfully.

1. Common relationship challenges

Relationship challenges can take various forms, including:

Conflicts: Disagreements and conflicts can arise due to differences of opinion, unmet needs, or misunderstandings.

Ineffective communication: Poor communication can lead to misunderstandings, frustrations, and tensions in a relationship.

Jealousy and boredom: In romantic relationships, jealousy and boredom can surface, testing trust and passion.

External stress: External pressures such as work, finances, or health can negatively influence a relationship.

Trust issues: Trust issues may emerge due to past events or current behaviors.

2. Tips for managing relationship challenges

Here are some tips for dealing with relationship challenges constructively:

Open communication: Communication is key. Talk openly about your concerns, needs, and feelings with the person involved.

Active listening: Listen attentively to the other person without interrupting. Try to understand their perspective before responding.

Empathy: Show empathy towards the other person. Try to see things from their point of view.

Conflict management: Learn conflict management techniques, such as problem-solving and negotiation, to resolve disagreements constructively.

Time for reflection: If emotions run high, take a step back to think before reacting impulsively.

Compromise: Be willing to make compromises to solve issues. Relationships often involve adjustments from both sides.

Solution-seeking: Focus on finding solutions rather than blame or guilt.

Stress management: If external stress is affecting your relationship, find ways to manage stress together, such as through exercise or meditation.

Seeking external help: If challenges persist, consider seeking the assistance of a counselor or couples therapist for professional support.

3. Relational challenges in romantic relationships

Romantic relationships often come with unique challenges. Here are some specific tips for managing relational challenges in this context:

Jealousy: Jealousy can be managed by strengthening communication and trust. Avoid overly possessive behaviors.

Routine and boredom: To overcome routine and boredom, plan exciting activities, getaways, or surprises to rekindle passion.

Emotional intimacy: Work on maintaining emotional intimacy by sharing your thoughts, dreams, and concerns.

Sexuality: If sexual issues arise, openly discuss them and consider seeking a sex therapist if necessary.

4. Relational challenges in professional relationships

Relational challenges at work can have a significant impact on your career and well-being. Here are some tips for managing them:

Professional communication: Adjust your communication based on the needs of your professional environment. Be clear and precise in your interactions.

Conflict management: Learn to handle workplace conflicts professionally, using problemsolving skills.

Collaboration: Encourage collaboration and teamwork to resolve issues and achieve goals.

Stress management: Use stress management techniques to stay calm and focused, even in stressful work situations.

5. Relationship challenges in social and family life

Social and family relationships can also present challenges. Here's how to manage them:

Family communication: Promote open communication within the family. Listen to family members and express your own feelings.

Managing family conflicts: Family conflicts can be delicate. Seek balanced solutions, and if necessary, consider family mediation.

Toxic friends: If you have toxic friends, consider distancing yourself or ending the relationship if it's harmful.

Part 7

The femme fatale at work and in social life

Chapter 18

The femme fatale at work

The femme fatale is not limited to her personal life; she also excels in her professional life. She embodies self-confidence, competence, and determination, making her not only seductive but also respected and admired in the professional world. We will explore how to become a femme fatale at work by developing skills, managing your career, and building strong professional relationships.

1. The femme fatale at work: a vision of excellence

The femme fatale at work is characterized by several essential traits:

Self-confidence: she has unwavering self-confidence, allowing her to make bold decisions and tackle challenges gracefully.

Competence: she excels in her field of work through her skills and her determination to constantly improve.

Emotional intelligence: she can handle professional relationships with finesse, understanding others' emotions and communicating effectively.

Leadership: she can lead a team with confidence, inspire others, and achieve ambitious goals.

2. Developing key skills

To become a femme fatale at work, it's essential to develop certain key skills:

Communication: Effective communication is crucial. Learn to express your ideas clearly, actively listen, and communicate tactfully.

Leadership: Develop leadership skills by learning to make informed decisions, inspire others, and manage a team.

Time management: Time management helps you stay organized and efficient. Prioritize, set goals, and manage your time wisely.

Stress management: Learn to manage workplace stress through relaxation techniques, meditation, and emotional management.

Problem-solving: Develop problem-solving skills to proactively address professional challenges.

3. Manage your career with confidence

A femme fatale at work manages her career with confidence and strategy. Here's how you can do it:

Professional goals: Set clear and ambitious professional goals. Having a long-term vision motivates you to progress.

Networking: Build a strong professional network by attending events, establishing connections, and seeking mentoring opportunities.

Continuous learning: Invest in your professional development by taking courses, reading relevant books, and staying up-to-date in your field.

Calculated risk-taking: Don't be afraid to take calculated risks to advance in your career. Success often lies outside your comfort zone.

Negotiation: Learn to negotiate effectively, whether it's for salary, benefits, or professional opportunities.

4. Build solid professional relationships

Solid professional relationships are essential for a successful career. Here's how to create and maintain such relationships:

Respect: Treat your colleagues, superiors, and subordinates with respect. Mutual consideration is the foundation of a healthy professional relationship.

Collaboration: Promote collaboration and teamwork. Share your skills and knowledge with others.

Active listening: Be an attentive listener. Listen to the needs and concerns of others and be open to communication.

Mutual assistance: Offer help when needed and ask for help when you need it. Mutual support strengthens relationships.

5. Managing professional challenges

Professional challenges can arise, but a femme fatale at work knows how to handle them gracefully:

Conflict management: Learn how to manage conflicts in the workplace constructively by using problem-solving and communication skills.

Mentorship: Seek out mentors and advice to guide you in your career.

Work-life balance: Balance your professional and personal life to avoid burnout and maintain your well-being.

Chapter 19

Networking with charisma

Networking with charisma is a valuable asset for any femme fatale, whether in her professional, social, or personal life. Charisma allows you to create authentic connections, positively influence others, and stand out in a world of interpersonal relationships. We will explore the principles of charisma and provide you with tips to develop this powerful quality.

1. Understanding charisma

Charisma is a magnetic quality that draws others towards you. It is based on self-confidence, presence, authenticity, and the ability to communicate in a captivating manner. Here's what charisma can bring you:

Influence: Charisma allows you to positively influence others and inspire them to follow your example.

Authentic connections: You can create authentic and meaningful connections with others, which strengthens your relationships.

Self-confidence: Charisma boosts your self-confidence as it reflects a positive self-acceptance.

Effective communication: You can communicate your ideas persuasively and captivatingly, enabling you to inspire and persuade others.

2. The principles of charisma

To develop charisma, it's helpful to understand the principles that underlie it:

Self-confidence: Self-confidence is the foundation of charisma. Believe in yourself, your abilities, and your worth.

Authenticity: Be authentic and genuine in your interactions with others. People are drawn to authenticity.

Active listening: Practice active listening by giving your full attention to the person you're talking to. Show interest in what they are saying.

Body language: Your body language plays a crucial role. Maintain a confident posture, make eye contact, and use expressive gestures.

Emotional expression: Express your emotions appropriately and sincerely. Charisma doesn't mean hiding your emotions but managing them maturely.

Storytelling: Tell captivating stories to illustrate your points and engage your audience.

3. Tips for networking with charisma

Here are some tips for networking with charisma and creating meaningful connections:

Presence: Be fully present in every interaction. Avoid mental distractions.

Smile: A warm smile can work wonders. It creates a positive atmosphere and invites others to get closer.

Positivity: Adopt a positive attitude. People are drawn to positive energy and avoid negative individuals.

Empathetic Listening: Listen to others with empathy. Try to understand their emotions and perspectives.

Engagement in the Conversation: Be engaged in the conversation. Ask relevant questions and show interest in the responses.

Personal Memory: Remember personal details that people share with you. It shows that you consider them important.

Mentoring: If you have skills or knowledge to share, consider becoming a mentor. Mentoring is an excellent way to develop professional relationships.

4. Charisma in professional networking

Charisma is particularly important in professional networking. Here's how to use it to your advantage:

Open approach: Approach new people with an open and welcoming attitude. Show interest in their work and goals.

Bridge-building: Find common ground with the people you meet. This makes it easier to establish connections.

Follow-up: After a professional encounter, follow up via email or phone to show ongoing interest.

Social media: Use social media strategically to expand your professional network and share your expertise.

Chapter 20

Being the star of social evenings

Social events offer a unique opportunity to shine and showcase your charisma in society. As a femme fatale, you can be the star of these events by attracting attention, creating meaningful connections, and leaving a memorable impression. We will explore strategies to shine at social events.

1. Preparation: the key to success

Preparation is essential to be the star of social events. Here are some important steps to follow before attending a social event:

Choose your outfit carefully: opt for an outfit that makes you feel confident and comfortable. Make sure it suits the type of event you're attending.

Practice conversation: think of interesting topics and questions to ask other guests. This will help you feel more prepared and create engaging interactions.

Know the event: research the event, its organizers, and its guests. Having information about the event can help you feel more at ease.

Self-confidence: cultivate self-confidence by recalling your achievements and practicing positive visualization.

2. Attract attention in a positive way

To be the star of social evenings, you need to attract positive attention. Here's how to do it:

Enter with confidence: When you arrive at the event, enter with confidence. Keep your head held high, smile, and make a memorable first impression.

Smile and eye contact: Use a warm smile and maintain eye contact when talking to others. This shows that you are open and interested.

Active listening: During conversations, practice active listening by giving your full attention to the person you're talking to. Ask relevant questions and show interest in their responses.

Share engaging stories: Tell engaging stories that pique the interest of others. Storytelling is an excellent way to create connections.

Spread positivity: Avoid complaining or speaking negatively. Instead, spread positivity and optimism.

3. Creating authentic connections

One of the keys to being the star of social evenings is to create authentic connections with other guests. Here's how to achieve that:

Ask open-ended questions: Ask open-ended questions that encourage others to share their thoughts and experiences.

Empathetic listening: Listen empathetically. Try to understand the emotions and perspectives of others.

Share personal experiences: Share your personal experiences authentically. This creates a deeper connection.

Sincere compliments: Give sincere compliments when you notice something positive about someone.

Follow-up: Follow up after the evening by sending a message or inviting the people you've connected with to meet up.

4. Be the centre of the party

To be the star of the social evening, you can adopt an attitude that allows you to shine more brightly:

Positive energy: bring positive energy to the party. Dance, laugh and encourage others to have fun.

Active participation: Don't be passive. Take an active part in the evening's activities, whether it's dancing, games or discussions.

Be adventurous: Be open to new experiences. Try activities you've never done before.

Make introductions: if you know people at the party, introduce them to the other guests. It shows you're sociable and willing to help.

5. Handling difficult conversations

Sometimes, you might encounter difficult conversations during social gatherings. Here's how to handle them gracefully:

Stay calm: Keep your composure, even if the conversation becomes tense. Avoid confrontations and seek common ground.

Change the subject: If the conversation veers into uncomfortable topics, subtly shift the subject to something positive.

Avoid negative individuals: If someone is negative or confrontational, politely distance yourself and seek more positive interactions.

Part 8

The femme fatale in love and romance

Chapter 21

The search for love

The search for love is a universal and essential quest in the lives of many femme fatales. While you may be confident and independent, finding authentic and fulfilling love can be a precious goal. We will explore how you can approach the search for love with confidence and emotional intelligence.

1. Understanding your desires and needs

The first step in seeking love is to understand your own desires and needs. Here are some questions to consider:

What are your love goals? Determine whether you are looking for a long-term relationship, an adventure, or something else.

What are your values and priorities? Identify the values that are important to you in a relationship, such as loyalty, communication, or stability.

What are your emotional needs? Reflect on what you need to feel fulfilled in a relationship, whether it's attention, emotional support, or understanding.

What are your selection criteria? Create a list of criteria that your potential partner should meet, keeping in mind that absolute perfection does not exist.

2. Self-confidence in the search for love

Self-confidence is a valuable asset when it comes to the search for love. Here's how you can apply it in this context:

Be open to meeting new people: have confidence in your ability to meet interesting and compatible individuals.

Express your needs: be confident in expressing your needs and expectations in a relationship while remaining open to communication.

Learn from past experiences: use self-confidence to learn from your past experiences and understand what you want in a relationship.

Don't underestimate yourself: don't settle for less than you deserve. Self-confidence helps you maintain high standards.

3. Communication in the search for love

Communication plays a crucial role in the search for love. Here's how you can use it effectively:

Express your intentions: Be clear about your intentions and expectations from the beginning of the relationship.

Empathetic listening: Actively listen to your potential partner to understand their needs and desires.

Conflict management: Learn to handle disagreements constructively to avoid misunderstandings.

Share your emotions: Be open to authentically sharing your emotions, which strengthens the emotional connection.

4. Patience and perseverance

The search for love can be a process that requires patience and perseverance. Don't rush into a relationship out of desperation, but instead look for a partnership that matches your values and needs. Here are a few tips on how to remain patient and persistent:

Don't rush: take the time to get to know your potential partner and develop a solid relationship before making a serious commitment.

Learn from disappointments: if you experience disappointments or break-ups, use them as learning opportunities to improve yourself in future relationships.

Expand your social circle: explore different avenues for meeting new people, whether online, through friends or by attending social events.

5. Balancing independence and commitment

As a femme fatale, you're probably independent and self-reliant. The balance between independence and commitment in a relationship can be tricky. Here's how to manage it:

Keep your independence: maintain your independence and continue to cultivate your own interests and passions.

Be open to commitment: Be open to commitment when you find someone who matches your values and needs.

Communicate your needs: make sure you communicate your needs for personal space and independence to your partner.

Chapter 22

Fulfilling love relationships

Fulfilling love relationships are an essential cornerstone in the life of a femme fatale. A strong and healthy relationship can bring joy, support, and a sense of fulfillment. We will explore the fundamental principles of fulfilling love relationships and how to nurture them for lasting happiness.

1. The foundations of fulfilling love relationships

Fulfilling love relationships are built on strong foundations. Here are some fundamental principles to keep in mind:

Open communication: Open and honest communication is essential. Share your thoughts, emotions, and concerns with your partner.

Mutual trust: Trust is the cornerstone of a healthy relationship. Be reliable and trustworthy to strengthen this mutual trust.

Respect: Respect your partner as an individual with their own needs, opinions, and aspirations. Mutual respect is non-negotiable.

Emotional support: Be an emotional support for each other, offering a safe space to express your emotions and being there in difficult times.

Independence and interdependence: Cultivate your personal independence while recognizing the importance of interdependence in a relationship. You are two distinct individuals who support each other.

2. Communication in fulfilling love relationships

Communication plays a central role in fulfilling romantic relationships. Here's how to use it to strengthen your relationship:

Active listening: practice active listening by giving your full attention to your partner when communicating. Avoid thinking about your response while the other person is speaking.

Express your needs and desires: be able to express your needs and desires clearly and respectfully. Don't assume that your partner should guess how you feel.

Avoid destructive criticism: if you have criticisms to make, do so in a constructive rather than a critical manner. Use "I" statements instead of "you" statements to express your feelings.

Conflict management: disagreements are inevitable, but learn to manage them respectfully. Seek solutions instead of blaming.

3. Personal and relational fulfillment

Fulfilling personal and relational development is essential in nurturing healthy and fulfilling romantic relationships. Here's how to maintain this balance:

Pursue your passions: Continue to pursue your personal passions and interests. This enriches your life and makes you more interesting to your partner.

Support each other's goals: Support your partner's personal goals and encourage them to achieve their dreams.

Quality time: Spend quality time together as a couple, but also allocate individual time for self-renewal.

Bonding: Create moments of bonding that strengthen your connection, such as going out together, having adventures, or simply spending quiet evenings at home.

4. Emotional and physical intimacy

Intimacy is a key element of fulfilling relationships and comes in two main forms:

Emotional intimacy: Share your emotions, fears, and dreams with your partner. Be a source of mutual support and a confidant.

Physical intimacy: Physical intimacy is important but should be based on respect and mutual consent. Communicate openly about your needs and boundaries.

Romance and passion: Don't forget to maintain passion and romance in your relationship. Create special moments that strengthen your connection.

5. Managing challenges in relationships

All relationships face challenges at some point. Here's how to successfully manage them:

Conflict resolution: Address conflicts constructively. Seek solutions together instead of pointing fingers.

Transitional periods: Transition periods, such as marriage, parenthood, or career changes, can be stressful. Communicate and plan these transitions together.

Support during tough times: Be there for your partner during difficult times. Offer emotional and practical support.

6. Self-love in a relationship

Self-love is essential in a fulfilling relationship. Make sure to maintain your self-esteem and not rely entirely on your partner for your happiness.

Self-esteem: continue to nurture a strong self-esteem. This makes you more attractive and helps you feel fulfilled in your relationship.

Independence: maintain your independence and continue to pursue your personal passions.

Self-respect: do not compromise your values or self-respect to please your partner. A healthy relationship is based on mutual respect.

Chapter 23

Maintaining a lasting passion

Maintaining a lasting passion is an essential component of a femme fatale's life. Whether it's for a career, a relationship, or a hobby, passion brings invaluable energy and fulfillment. We will explore strategies for cultivating and nurturing a passion that endures over time.

1. The quest for passion

Passion is a powerful force that gives meaning to life. However, it doesn't always manifest naturally. Here's how you can embark on a quest for your passion:

Exploration: Be open to exploring different activities, as you may not immediately know what truly passionate about.

Listen to yourself: Pay attention to your intuitions and emotions to identify what piques your interest and enthusiasm.

Identify your strengths: Recognize your natural strengths and talents. Your passion may be related to what you excel at.

Set goals: Establish clear goals for your passion quest. This will provide you with a sense of direction.

2. Developing passion

Once you've identified your passion, it's essential to develop and keep it alive. Here's how to do it:

Commitment: Fully commit to your passion. Dedicate time and energy to its development.

Continuous Learning: Stay open to continuous learning in the field of your passion. The more you know, the more passionate you'll become.

Overcome Obstacles: Expect to encounter obstacles along the way. Identify them and seek solutions to overcome them.

Creativity: Express your creativity within your passion. Look for new ways to explore and enjoy it.

3. Passion in your career

To maintain passion in your career, here are some helpful tips:

Find your calling: Seek a career that aligns with your interests, skills, and values.

Set professional goals: Establish challenging professional goals that give you a long-term sense of purpose.

Balance: Maintain a work-life balance to prevent burnout.

Reinvention: Be open to professional reinvention if your passion evolves over time.

4. Passion in relationships

Passion in relationships is crucial to keep them alive. Here's how to maintain that passion:

Special evenings: Plan special evenings with your partner to reignite the flame of passion.

Express your feelings: Openly express your feelings and desire for your partner.

Adventure: Seek new experiences to share together to create exciting memories.

Communication: Communicate openly about your relationship needs and desires.

5. Passion in hobbies

Hobbies are an excellent way to cultivate passion in your life. Here are some tips to maintain this passion:

Diversity: Explore a variety of hobbies to discover what passions you the most.

Commitment: Dedicate regular time to your hobbies to keep them alive.

Sharing: If possible, share your hobbies with others who have the same interests.

Challenges: Seek challenges in your hobbies to stay motivated and passionate.

6. Resilience in passion

Passion can be tested by challenges and obstacles. Here's how to maintain resilience in your passion:

Persevere: don't be discouraged by setbacks. Perseverance is essential to maintaining passion.

Learn from failures: see failures as learning opportunities. They can help you grow and evolve in your passion.

Remain open to change: your passion can evolve over time. Be open to new directions.

Find support: look for support from people who share your passion or mentors who can guide you.

Part 9

Overcoming obstacles

Chapter 24

Overcoming complexes and fears

All women, even the most confident and alluring ones, have insecurities and fears. These feelings can hinder your growth as a femme fatale. We will explore strategies to identify, understand, and overcome your insecurities and fears, allowing you to shine even brighter.

1. Identify complexes and fears

The first step in overcoming insecurities and fears is to identify them. Here are some questions to help you reflect on these feelings:

What aspects of yourself do you dislike or find imperfect? Identify the parts of yourself that evoke feelings of insecurity.

What situations or challenges make you feel fear or insecurity? Examine the moments when you feel least confident.

When did these insecurities and fears begin to manifest in your life? Identify past experiences that may have contributed to their development.

2. Understanding the origins of complexes and fears

Once you've identified your insecurities and fears, try to understand their origins. Often, these feelings have deep roots in your past. Here's how to explore this origin:

Self-reflection: Take time to reflect on your past and the experiences that may have contributed to the formation of your insecurities and fears.

Consult a professional: If your insecurities and fears are deeply rooted and are preventing you from living fully, consider seeing a psychologist or counselor. They can help you explore these feelings in depth.

Confide in a trusted friend: Talk about your feelings with a trusted friend or family member. Sometimes, discussing these emotions can help you better understand them.

3. Change your inner narrative

Complexes and fears are often linked to a negative inner narrative. You can change this narrative to encourage yourself instead of sabotaging yourself. Here's how to do it:

Practice self-compassion: Be kind and compassionate to yourself. Speak to yourself as you would to a loving friend.

Identify negative thoughts: Become aware of the negative thoughts that fuel your complexes and fears. Once you spot them, replace them with positive and realistic thoughts.

Affirm your worth: Remember that you have intrinsic value as a human being. Your worth is not dependent on your appearance or success.

Positive visualization: Practice positive visualization by imagining situations in which you feel confident and succeed. This will boost your self-confidence.

4. Gradual exposure

Gradual exposure is a technique that involves progressively confronting your fears and insecurities. Here's how to apply it:

Identify a fear or insecurity: Choose a specific fear or insecurity you want to overcome.

Start small: Begin with mildly uncomfortable situations, and then gradually progress to more intimidating ones.

Celebrate victories: Celebrate every small victory, regardless of its size. This will boost your self-confidence.

Persevere: Expect challenging moments, but persevere. Perseverance is the key to overcoming your fears.

5. Self-acceptance

Self-acceptance is an essential element in overcoming insecurities and fears. Here's how to integrate it into your life:

Be yourself: Accept yourself as you are, with all your imperfections. No one is perfect, and that's what makes each person unique.

Celebrate your strengths: Focus on your strengths and positive qualities. You have many qualities worth celebrating.

Avoid comparison: Steer clear of comparing yourself to others. Everyone has their own path and challenges.

Cultivate gratitude: Practice gratitude by focusing on the positive aspects of your life. This can help alleviate feelings of insecurity and fear.

Chapter 25

Dealing with rejection and adversity

Rejection and adversity are inevitable aspects of life, even for the most confident and resilient femme fatales. Knowing how to deal with these challenges is essential to maintain your self-confidence and determination. We will explore strategies for managing rejection and adversity with grace and resilience.

1. Understanding rejection

Rejection can take many forms, whether in relationships, career, or other aspects of life. Here's how to understand and handle it:

Accepting emotions: When you face rejection, it's normal to feel sadness, anger, or disappointment. Accept these emotions as a natural response.

Not taking it personally: Rejection isn't necessarily an indication of your personal worth. It can be related to external circumstances or personal preferences.

Learning from experiences: See rejection as a learning opportunity. Try to understand what you can take away from it to improve yourself.

Long-term perspective: Keep in mind that rejection is often a step towards a better opportunity. What may seem like a short-term loss can be a long-term gain.

2. Resilience in the face of adversity

Adversity can be a major challenge in life. Here's how to develop resilience to face adversity:

Adjust your attitude: Adopt a positive and proactive attitude towards adversity. See challenges as opportunities for growth.

Find support: Seek support from friends, family, or a professional if needed. Talking about your difficulties can help you overcome them.

Develop coping mechanisms: Learn healthy coping mechanisms to manage stress and adversity, such as meditation, exercise, or writing. Coping involves a set of behaviors, thoughts, and emotions to handle stress and pressure in a more adaptive way.

Set realistic goals: Establish realistic goals to deal with adversity. Break down significant challenges into more manageable steps.

3. Handling rejections in relationships

Rejection in relationships can be particularly challenging to handle. Here are some tips for dealing with rejection in this context:

Communicate openly: If you're rejected in a relationship, try to communicate openly to understand the reasons behind this decision.

Take a step back: Take emotional distance to evaluate the relationship and determine if it was truly in line with your needs and values.

Learn from the experience: Use rejection as an opportunity to learn about yourself and what you're looking for in a relationship.

Remain open to new encounters: Don't let rejection discourage you from seeking love. Stay open to new encounters.

4. Managing career rejections

Rejection in one's career can be disheartening, but it is often unavoidable. Here's how to handle it professionally:

Seek feedback: If you face rejection for a professional opportunity, ask for constructive feedback to improve your skills.

Keep networking: Stay active in professional networking, as new opportunities can arise at any time.

Highlight your strengths: Focus on your strengths and unique skills to stand out in your career.

Don't lose confidence: A professional rejection should not undermine your confidence in your abilities. Keep believing in yourself.

5. Managing rejections in hobbies

Hobbies can be a source of pleasure, but they can also involve rejection if you don't always succeed as you wish. Here's how to manage rejection in your hobbies:

Enjoyment perspective: Remember that hobbies are primarily for your enjoyment. Don't put too much pressure on performance.

Learn from failure: Use failures in your hobbies as an opportunity to learn and improve.

Stay open to creativity: Hobbies are a space where you can express your creativity without fearing the judgment of others.

Explore new horizons: If a hobby no longer brings you joy, explore new horizons to find something that truly excites you.

Chapter 26

Maintaining a persistent attitude

Persistence is one of the most valuable qualities to become a femme fatale. A persistent attitude allows you to overcome obstacles, reach your goals, and become the best version of yourself. We'll explore how to maintain a persistent attitude to succeed in all aspects of your life.

1. Understanding persistence

Persistence is the ability to persevere despite difficulties, setbacks, and obstacles. It relies on determination, resilience, and the will to pursue your goals even when things get tough. Here's how to understand persistence:

Have a clear goal: Persistence is easier when you have a clear goal in mind. Define what you want to achieve clearly.

Overcome obstacles: Expect to encounter obstacles on your path. Persistence involves overcoming them rather than avoiding them.

Learn from failure: Failure is a natural step toward success. Use every failure as a learning opportunity.

Maintain motivation: Find sources of motivation that remind you why you're pursuing your goals.

2. Developing persistence

Persistence can be cultivated and strengthened over time. Here's how to develop this quality:

Develop resilience: resilience helps you cope with setbacks and come back stronger. Work on your emotional and mental resilience.

Manage your time: effective time management keeps you persistent by helping you stay focused on your goals.

Stay flexible: persistence doesn't necessarily mean staying on the same track at all costs. Be open to adjusting your approach if necessary.

Find support: surround yourself with people who support and encourage you in your perseverance.

3. Career persistence

Persistence is particularly crucial in the professional field. Here's how to maintain a persistent attitude in your career:

Set professional goals: Establish clear and ambitious professional goals. This will give you a direction to follow.

Continued learning: Be open to continuous learning to improve your skills and stay competitive.

Handle rejections: Expect rejections in your career, but don't let them discourage you. Use them as opportunities for improvement.

Networking: Professional networking can open new doors in your career. Be persistent in your efforts to establish contacts.

4. Persistence in relationships

Persistence can also be applied in relationships. Here's how to maintain a persistent attitude in this context:

Communicate openly: Persistence in relationships involves open and honest communication. Don't let misunderstandings accumulate.

Overcome conflicts: Expect conflicts in relationships, but seek to resolve them rather than avoid them.

Be consistent: Persistence in relationships means being consistent in your commitment to your partner.

Learn and grow: Relationships evolve over time. Be persistent in your willingness to learn and grow together.

5. Persistence in hobbies

Persistence in your hobbies can bring you great satisfaction. Here's how to maintain it:

Regular practice: Be persistent in practicing your hobbies to develop your skills.

Explore new horizons: If a hobby becomes boring, be open to trying new ones to maintain your interest.

Share your passions: Share your passions with others who have similar interests. This can strengthen your commitment.

Seek challenges: Look for challenges in your hobbies to maintain your motivation and persistence.

6. Persistence in your transformation into a femme fatale

Persistence is particularly important in your transformation into a femme fatale. Here's how to maintain it throughout this journey:

Stay committed: Remain committed to your transformation, even when faced with challenges.

Learn from your experiences: Use every step of your transformation as a learning opportunity.

Stay true to yourself: Be persistent in your authenticity. Don't change who you are to please others.

Celebrate progress: Celebrate each step of your transformation. This will boost your motivation.

Part 10

An empowered femme fatale

Chapter 27

Balancing personal and professional life

Balancing personal and professional life is essential for a femme fatale striving for success and well-being. This balance allows you to excel in your career while maintaining healthy relationships and a fulfilling quality of life. We will explore strategies to find this delicate balance.

1. Understanding Balance

Balancing personal and professional life involves finding the right middle ground between your professional commitments and personal needs. Here's how to understand this balance:

Clear priorities: Identify your priorities in life. What matters most to you personally and professionally?

Redefining success: Redefine your concept of success to include personal well-being and relationships, in addition to professional achievements.

Time management: Learn to effectively manage your time to allocate quality time to each aspect of your life.

Flexibility: Be open to adjusting your schedule based on the changing needs of your life.

2. Developing balance

Balancing personal and professional life can be cultivated and improved. Here's how to develop this balance:

Strategic planning: Create a plan that integrates your professional and personal goals, allocating time to each area.

Self-care: Take care of yourself physically and mentally. Self-care strengthens your ability to handle challenges.

Disconnect: Learn to disconnect from work when you're off duty. Avoid checking your work emails outside of working hours.

Social support: Surround yourself with people who support your quest for balance and can assist you in times of need.

3. Balancing career and personal life

Finding the balance between your career and your personal life can be a challenge, but it's essential for your overall well-being. Here's how to maintain this balance:

Set boundaries: Establish clear boundaries between your work and personal life. Respect these boundaries as much as possible.

Plan quality time: Reserve quality time for your loved ones and hobbies. Plan special activities to strengthen your relationships.

Prioritize health: Neglecting your physical and mental health can compromise your balance. Prioritize your well-being.

Learn to say no: Don't overload yourself with work responsibilities. Learn to say no when necessary to preserve your balance.

4. Balancing relationships and career

Maintaining healthy relationships while succeeding in your career is a delicate balance. Here's how to achieve it:

Communicate: openly communicate with your partner, family, and friends about your professional commitments and personal time needs.

Plan special moments: schedule special moments with your loved ones to strengthen your bonds, even if you have a busy schedule.

Flexibility: be flexible in managing your schedule to meet the needs of your relationships.

Clear priorities: make sure your loved ones understand your professional priorities, as well as the importance of your personal life.

5. Balancing hobbies and career

Hobbies are an essential component of your personal life. Here's how to balance them with your career:

Schedule time for hobbies: Set aside regular time for your hobbies to maintain your personal fulfillment.

Integrate hobbies: If possible, integrate your hobbies into your professional life by choosing activities that enhance your skills or creativity.

Manage stress: Hobbies can be a welcome escape from work-related stress. Use them as a means of relaxation.

Be present: When engaging in your hobbies, be fully present and fully committed.

Chapter 28

The well-being and health of the femme fatale

Being a femme fatale goes far beyond appearance and seduction. It also involves taking care of your well-being and health. We will explore the importance of well-being and health for the femme fatale, as well as strategies to maintain a healthy balance in your life.

1. The importance of well-being and health

Well-being and health are the foundations of your success as a femme fatale. They influence all aspects of your life, from your self-confidence to your ability to achieve your goals. Here's why they are so important:

Self-confidence: Good physical and mental health enhance your self-confidence, which is essential for seduction and success.

Energy and vitality: Being in good health gives you the energy and vitality needed to shine in your career and relationships.

Resilience: Good mental health helps you face challenges with resilience, which is essential for overcoming obstacles.

Appearance: Taking care of your physical well-being contributes to a radiant and seductive appearance.

2. Strategies for well-being and health

Maintaining your well-being and health is an investment in your success as a femme fatale. Here are strategies to achieve this:

Balanced diet: Adopt a balanced diet rich in fruits, vegetables, lean proteins, and whole grains. Avoid excess sugar, salt, and saturated fats.

Regular exercise: Incorporate a regular exercise routine into your life. Exercise strengthens your body, boosts your energy, and improves your mental well-being.

Quality sleep: Prioritize quality sleep. Good rest is essential for physical and mental recovery.

Stress management: Learn stress management techniques such as meditation, deep breathing, and relaxation to maintain emotional balance.

Regular health check-ups: Schedule regular health check-ups to detect potential health issues at an early stage.

Personal development: Invest in your personal development by reading, taking courses, and seeking continuous self-improvement.

Work-life balance: Ensure you maintain a healthy balance between your career and personal life. Don't neglect your personal needs.

Self-confidence: Working on your self-esteem and self-confidence is essential for your mental well-being.

3. The mental health of the femme fatale

Mental health is a critical aspect of the well-being of the femme fatale. Here's how to take care of your mental health:

Stress management: Learn to effectively manage stress to prevent mental health issues.

Meditation and mindfulness: Practice meditation and mindfulness to maintain emotional balance.

Social support: Surround yourself with positive and supportive people who can assist you in challenging times.

Therapy: Don't hesitate to consult a mental health professional if you need support in dealing with emotional issues.

4. The physical well-being of the femme fatale

The physical well-being is also essential. Here's how to take care of it:

Healthy eating: adopt a balanced diet that nourishes your body and enhances your inner and outer beauty.

Regular exercise: incorporate exercise into your daily routine to maintain your physical fitness and vitality.

Quality sleep: prioritize restful sleep for body regeneration.

Skin and hair care: take care of your skin and hair to maintain a radiant appearance

Table of contents